Ndestructible 7
Mental Well-Being Playbook

Ndestructible 7
Mental Well-Being Playbook:

Growing older isn't for wimps!

Lenore Lawson Doster, MA, PsyD

XULON PRESS

Xulon Press
555 Winderley Pl, Suite 225
Maitland, FL 32751
407.339.4217
www.xulonpress.com

Paperback ISBN-13: 978-1-66288-115-2
Ebook ISBN-13: 978-1-66288-116-9

Dedication & Acknowledgements

To the *Ndestructible 7* Mental Wellness Life Coaches. May God bless you and the hard work you are doing. May the Lord continue to give you much guidance from above!

To my sister-in-law, Dr. Deborah Doster Viglione, an integrative and internal medicine specialist. Thank you for all you do for so many, including my family! You are an inspirational warrior in the medical field, devoted to excellence and advancement. I am certain God is grateful for your service! May God continue to be with you, blessing your courage and your work.

In memory of those who have gone before us. To my departed family: Jerry Lawson (Dad), Elaine Lawson (Mom), June Doster (mother-in-law), Matt Lawson (brother), Mark Lawson (brother), Catherine Lawson (sister), Mark Richardson (brother-in-law), Ron Rowe (brother-in-law), Dwaine Rowe (nephew), Bob Marken ("uncle-in-law"), Bette Marken ("aunt-in-law"), and Dave Wiedemann (mentor).

And lastly, a special acknowledgement to Harold Doster, my father-in-law, age ninety-two! Way to go, Hal!

With Sincere Appreciation

With sincere gratitude to Don Doster, my great husband and partner. One of the first *Ndestructible 7* Life Coaches. Thank you for stepping up on this Ndestructible journey! It was through your encouragement and interactions that made this guidebook a reality.

To Hunter Doster my son. Thank you for always being willing to take my calls, providing love, support, wisdom, and fun. Being the lone survivor of multiple rounds of in vitro we experienced in 1996–1998! It has certainly been a joy to witness your adventurous life. Never a dull moment!

To the memory of Ken Shumard, who passed away on Valentine's Day 2023. Thank you for being a wonderful CEO and giving us, as well as many others, the chance to have children of our own. In the mid-1990s, Ken stepped up and purchased in-vitro insurance for several of his employees, an expensive form of insurance that his company, Medical Doctor Associates (MDA), could not afford. But that didn't matter to Ken, a man who, as my husband says, "Didn't follow the worldly playbook of CEOs!" He leaped out in faith, providing this assistance. MDA became a wildly successful company.

You can find out more about Ken Shumard and all the incredible things he's done through the Ken Shumard Foundation.[1]

And thank you to all the Pentecostal pastors, who step-up in so many ways, including my amazing pastor, Jentezen Franklin. He doesn't personally know me yet. My prayer is that he will soon. I did have the benefit of hopping into his line for anointing at the end of the 9 a.m. service on March 5, 2023. When placing his hands on my forehead and the back of my head, he said, "You can slay it ... You already have it!" Wow, this came on the heels of me debating and looking for signs as to whether or not the *Ndestructible 7* playbook was ready to roll out. That message settled things for me. I took this as a "Yes!" So, no more waiting; I'm taking the leap and publishing this roadmap through Xulon Press. I'm curious to see where the Lord takes this *Ndestructible 7* guidebook and its leaders. And prayers for Pastor Franklin, for his ministry, safety, and health.

Credits:

Editing, Wordsmithing & Design: Xulon Press Team
Content Strategy: Regina Riedel
Images: www.shutterstock.com

---

[1] (https://www.causeiq.com/organizations/
the-shumard-foundation,203798084/)

Preface

Four days ago, my husband, Don, received the results back from his computerized tomography scan, also known as a CT scan. The results came back positive for an aortic aneurysm and other pulmonary complications. Frightening!

It's around 4 a.m. right now, and I am wide-awake, lying in bed with a heavy heart. A cascade of emotions are running through me, including angst, dread, grief, and deflation! At the same time, there's the coping in play that I've come to appreciate and count on as my *Ndestructible 7*.

The valuable *Ndestructible 7* weaponry was an inspiration from the Lord that I acquired over the years while serving clients in my psychology practice. I'm certainly leaning on the Lord right now, Who I sense is nearby. I'm having good connections, especially with our son, Hunter, receiving support and care from my kind loved ones and friends, managing my emotional turmoil by calling to the Wise Mind for direction, thinking about the next possible steps and routines that make sense, and utilizing inner character, such as fortitude and faith, to weather this storm.

I'm especially grateful for the spiritual impression the Lord sent me on March 10, 2023, three days prior to the CT scan revealing Don's aneurysm and blood clot.

This particular day, it was just after 11 a.m. I was taking some moments of quiet time and reflection. I picked up the Kingdom Connection Daily Devotional for March–May 2023 by Jentezen Franklin.[1] While reviewing the March three-part series called, "When God sends you an angel," I was grateful for angels that had come into my life. I even sent a text to an individual, "Creasy," who was definitely an angel to me during a challenging time in my life. So, I was in a spirit of belief that God could send an angel to help Don, who hadn't been feeling well for at least the six months prior.

Yes, six months! Over those months, Don had endured things such as another round of COVID-19, two episodes of pneumonia, a surgery, and multiple chest X-rays—too long to explain further now. He was following all his doctors' orders, including taking numerous medications and supplements. Yet, he was still feeling terrible. On March 10, while seated on a stool at our kitchen island, it popped into my mind that Don needed "a more thorough and updated medical review." I took this as a spiritual impression.

A spiritual impression is something that is formed without conscious thought, usually coming in the form of an idea, feeling, or opinion about something or someone. While sharing the impression with Don, it occurred to me that I could reach out to a nearby independent imaging center that I had used before for a knee issue I was having. They allowed for self-referral.

So, I made the call. The kind staff member heard my story, and although she didn't feel an MRI was the route to go, she recommended a CT scan. Unfortunately, their center didn't do CT scanning. She gave me information about another local imaging center that did that kind of work.

I contacted the recommended center, and another attentive staff member stated that they had quick openings and walked me through what I needed to do to proceed. The challenge was that the process starts with a doctor referral, which wasn't going to be easy because several of our local doctors were difficult, if not impossible, to contact. Their staff and procedures just simply weren't like the previous two ladies who quickly took my call and were willing to go the extra yard—this is another long story of which I will spare you the details. However, if a CT scan was what the Lord was guiding us to do, I was determined to get it done somehow, someway.

The CT was ordered by Don's sister Debbie. Debbie is an accomplished integrative internal medicine physician and one of the individuals whom I dedicated this workbook. She has served as an angel of health for so many, including him. Debbie is always quickly willing to step-up and serve. She's one of God's great humans, that's for sure! Clearly, she was the angel prescribing the correct tests that detected Don's serious health complications of which we now have the opportunity to treat. It appears that God has been sending Don several angels. Still, where things stand today, we remain in a race against the clock in the "hurry up and wait" routine of trying to get further medical care–starting with a well grounded treatment plan–before a rupture or dissection.

I'm currently hopeful and praying. At the same time, I'm fully aware of the various results that can come from these types of circumstances.

Fortunately, I have the *Ndestructible 7* weapons that have served me well so far! I am grateful. This artillery offers me hope and contentment in the midst of this ordeal and for the road forward.

I'm ready for what's in front of me. Uncertain, but prepared.

Back to you. Ahead in this guidebook, you will find an arsenal of weapons to help you manage what comes your way. Experiencing all things with contentment and living life to the fullest is the reward of a *Ndestructible 7* Warrior!

This playbook is my gift to you. *Ndestructible 7* is a roadmap through life's trials; a guide that I know you will come to appreciate as I do right now.

So, armor-up and soar through the upcoming chapters of your life! And pay attention to those winks and nudges from above!

-Lenore Doster, March 2023

Armor-up for Renewal: Ndestructible™ 7

Ready, Lord, to put off my old ways and fix my eyes on what is better;
to turn away from the **e**nvironment that weighed me down and broke me;
to walk with **n**ew habits that will build me up;
to let **e**verlasting experiences and excellent character rest on my shoulders;
to allow my **w**isdom to win and shield me from further harm;
to let others equip me and hold me **a**ccountable;
to reach out in acts of **l**ove toward others and myself.

Table of Contents

Introduction

Growing Older Isn't for Wimps: Optimize Life's Next Chapter with Ndestructible 7 *Rock Solid Mental Wellness!*

"I f we change, things change!" This is the theory behind *Ndestructible 7*.

Growing older is not for wimps! Chunks will be taken out of you in this life. All of us have battles to face; it's how we respond that makes all the difference.

In 2008, I published *Rock Solid Parenting: Secrets of an Effective Parent.*[2] In the introduction, I asked readers to consider the need to develop a strategic plan to guide their child through high school. I asked the readers to assume that every good coach has a game plan.

Every business owner has a business plan. Corporations have strategic plans. Colleges and universities have all sorts of operating plans for students, faculty, staff, and facilities. Similarly, every parent needs a good parenting plan!

Well, now it's time to zero in and double-check to make sure you have a rock solid plan for maintaining your own mental health.

So, that's the foundation we're looking to build. Now, let's talk about the tools. In the sections ahead, you will find details about the seven crucial elements of the Ndestructible

R.E.N.E.W.A.L. process. Each chapter provides foundational principles and targets to aim for. These targets will help you suit up with the necessary armor to win the battle and maximize your own mental health.

Armor-up! Hit the targets!

"Put on the full armor of God, so that when the day of evil comes, you may be able to stand your ground, and after you have done everything, stand."

- Ephesians 6:13

Through this process, you will be developing a "mental health toolbox." When setting up any ordinary toolbox for your home, certain tools are staples. Things like a hammer or a trusty set of screwdrivers are must-haves. The same is true of our *Ndestructible 7* Mental Health Toolbox. There are a particular set of weapons to keep handy that help us take command over life's troubles.

The Ndestructible R.E.N.E.W.A.L. process gives us these tools and a framework of seven essential targets for making the most of the next chapters of your life. They are:

- R–Becoming READY to clean up any brokenness and to reclaim your true spirit

- E–Constructing the right ENVIRONMENT and making any necessary changes

- N–Adopting NEW healthy habits and replacing self-defeating ones

- E–Creating EVERLASTING experiences and character

- W–Letting your WISDOM win and be your guide

- A–Embracing ACCOUNTABILITY and allowing others to sharpen you

- L–Doing LOVING actions for yourself, others, and your community

Each of the seven steps of the Ndestructible R.E.N.E.W.A.L. process offers us another piece of that armor. Adopting them all in total provides that "full armor" that protects our mental well-being and empowers us to thrive. Together, these steps are the "Ndestructible 7" of rock solid mental renewal and the path to a better life.

Throughout this playbook, you will find areas to record personal notes and reflections. See it as an opportunity to coach yourself; jotting down those essential reminders to keep you energized and focused on your targets for growth and mental wellness. Essentially, to design your personal Ndestructible 7 mental well-being game plan to a better you!

Ready to face the coming chapters of your life with passion and purpose? Bring your spirit of belief and come with us as we explore the process of Ndestructible R.E.N.E.W.A.L. and how it can put you on the right course to choose what is best for your emotional wellness right now!

Notes to Myself:

Chapter 1

Beginning the Warrior Journey: Getting Started with the Right Spirit!

> *"Do not be anxious about anything, but in every situation, by prayer and petition, with thanksgiving, present your requests to God. And the peace of God, which transcends all understanding, will guard your hearts and your minds in Christ Jesus." -Philippians 4:6-7*

B attles in life are inevitable. Life brings emotional bumps and bruises.

You are the best person to look after yourself. Protect yourself! This is accomplished best by anchoring yourself to the greatest resources.

With the seven targets for mental R.E.N.E.W.A.L., we have what we need to maintain strong mental well-being. Why am I emphasizing "maintaining" or "reclaiming" solid mental health? Because mental health is not a privilege. "Crazy" doesn't just disappear. Mental wellness is like anything else that you have to maintain.

Maintaining physical health requires proper nutrition and exercise. We must do the same thing for our overall emotional well-being. To ensure the highest probability of sustaining mental health, we must track and implement key behavioral, environmental, emotional, and cognitive patterns and habits. In other words, "put on the full armor of God."

Ndestructible 7 allows us to armor-up! It is a unique blend of spirituality, behavioral science, and life experience. It's an existential process for tackling life's issues and suffering; where we maintain a focus on mental well-being, no matter what is thrown at us.

We begin the *Ndestructible 7* journey by having faith and being in the right spirit. Therefore, the *Ndestructible 7* Warrior groups begin with prayer. Our prayer aligns us to the spiritual realm; specifically, connecting us to the Mighty Warrior and the Holy Spirit!

> *"Now faith is the substance of things hoped for,*
> *the evidence of things not seen."*
> *(Hebrews 11:11)*

So, whether you are in a group, at a retreat, by yourself, or with a recovery partner, you can begin by armoring up through prayer. Using the *Ndestructible 7 Covenant Commitment* and the *Armor-up for Renewal: Ndestructible 7* prayer.

Let us pray …

Ndestructible™ 7 Covenant Commitment: Forging a great suit of armor!

There are times when I'm at my best. There are times when I'm at my worst. I will handle the baggage I've been carrying. I will prepare for the troubles ahead. I will learn what is best for my well-being here and now. I will armor myself to improve my situation. I will reach for the stars, receive winks from above, and partner with the Holy Spirit. I will hit my targets. I will have a new story!

Armor-up for Renewal: Ndestructible™ 7

Ready, Lord, to put off my old ways and fix my eyes on what is better;

to turn away from the **e**nvironment that weighed me down and broke me;

to walk with **n**ew habits that will build me up;

to let **e**verlasting experiences and excellent character rest on my shoulders;

to allow my **w**isdom to win and shield me from further harm;

to let others equip me and hold me **a**ccountable;

to reach out in acts of **l**ove toward others and myself.

Notes to Myself:

Chapter 2

Start Hitting the Targets! Ndestructible 7 Target #1: Ready to Fix My Eyes on What's Better for the Next Chapter of My Life!

Armor Up & Hit Target #1!
"Put on the full armor of God." – Ephesians 6:13

◎ *Target 1 Reflection*

How are you feeling at the moment?

- Do you think your mind is sharp?

- Are you hopeful about the future?

- Can you take on adversity and stress with clarity?

- Can you manage your emotions and act quickly and decisively?

- Do you trust your ability to make beneficial decisions?

- Is your life manageable?

- Can you engage with others in a loving, effective manner?

There are times when we're at our best. There are times when we're at our worst.

Imagine your eyes are opening and it's another day. You experience the usual early-morning haze. The familiar weight of what has been haunting you is still there. In the past, you were hoping the problems would fade, and yet, they persist.

Maybe you're experiencing specific struggles. There's brokenness inside of you causing destruction that you haven't been able to leave behind. Perhaps it is past baggage you have been carrying around for years like a heavy suitcase. It could be the unresolved strain of a relationship that is impossible for you to ignore. It could be out-of-control substance use that's burdened you for years. It might be an avalanche of emotions rushing through you that you cannot seem to regulate, or you're drowning in emotional eating or some other coping problem that you've been hiding.

No question, there are moments in all our lives when we are driven to our knees.

Making a conscious choice to change is a real, necessary, and a crucial first phase of the process. The consequences can be devastating when we simply let problems linger and fail to take action. For example, emotional eating can quickly escalate to excessive weight gain and health problems. Substance abuse can lead to neglect of one's family. Out-of-control anxiety can create job performance issues. It is important to reiterate that some issues, like chronic health problems or catastrophic injuries, won't disappear. However, even with chronic conditions, we can often make adjustments that help us manage or improve our situation.

The "how to" of change can be the tricky part that prevents us from being ready to change. So many times, we say, *"I need to change this or that,"* but we aren't specific. For example, some comments in therapy are very general, such as *"I want to cope better," "I want happiness," "I want to be less anxious,"* or *"I want confidence."* These generic comments are a recognition of the need to change, but to have a better chance for success, we really need a more detailed process.

Correctly framing the change you desire is like the visor of your armor's helmet; it brings clarity of vision that empowers you to create a better next chapter of life. The exercises below will help you clearly frame the change you are needing.

See it! Frame it! Claim it!

◎ *Exercises for Target 1:*

Pause for a moment. Make sure you are in a comfortable, private space so you can have a moment of reflection. Breath in and out. Pay attention to your breathing. Be determined to start this journey. Follow the outline below. To make this experience more real, read the statements, declarations, and questions out loud. Pause periodically to have a conversation with yourself; speak your answers so that you can hear yourself.

- Is there something that's been haunting you, holding you back, burdening you, or would simply make your life better to be without?

- Ask yourself: *"Is there something I need at this time of my life? Is there something I need for a better next chapter?"*

- For example, do you want: to weather your current life transition better; to manage a relationship better; to manage your emotions better; to be more effective at your work; to take care of yourself better; to resolve inner bitterness/resentment; to be content with your circumstances; to resolve a past hurt?

- When you are deciding, here's a hint: Our symptoms speak our needs—for example, grief signals hurt and the need for comfort; anger signals a need to resolve helplessness and the need to gain empowerment; depression signals haplessness and the need to bring hope/faith/joy/contentment; burnout signals being overwhelmed

and the need for rejuvenation/refreshment/regener-
ation, etc.

- Ask yourself: *"If I continue down this same path, where will I be in one to three years in my personal, relational, and/or work life? Where will I be if I go down another path of meeting my target, needs, and wishes?"*

Notes to Myself:

◎ *Next Exercises for Target 1:*

- Select an item to address and frame the action in a concise manner that describes what you want. For example, *"I want to reduce my anxiety when public speaking and instead have fun when I do work presentations."*

- Seek something attractive to aim for; make commitments such as, *"I'm not going to get pushed around, I'm going to be assertive!"* or *"I'm going to stop being overwhelmed by learning to set boundaries and say no!"*

- Add a spiritual principle that will ground you — principles such as, *"I'm going to reduce my worries by staying in the moment and letting today's troubles be enough for today (Mat. 6:34),"* or *"I will be more peaceful and content regardless of the amount of stress I face each day running my business (Phil. 4:12–13)."*

- At some point in the future, consider voicing your action item to a trusted, wise friend.

Notes to Myself:

◎ *Final Reflection for Target 1:*

Now go a step further in your consideration of your action item/goal/target for an even better chance of success in overcoming it! Begin to think about it using the "S.M.A.R.T." strategy below:

S.M.A.R.T. strategy

- S.M.A.R.T. is a mnemonic acronym that gives us the criteria needed to set our objectives. As coined in the early 1980s by George T. Doran, a consultant and former director of corporate planning for Washington Water Power Company, it stands for: Specific, Measurable, Achievable, Realistic, and Time-bound.[3]

- Today, the strategy is often applied in the corporate world in project management, employee performance management, and personal development.[4] But the universal wisdom of S.M.A.R.T. objectives makes the approach easily applicable to many of the challenges in our daily lives.

Let's look at the concept of **S.M.A.R.T. Change** by using an example from the challenge my husband and I faced during the 2008 recession. At the time, my husband co-owned a private health and wellness business consulting company. After September 15, he lost 90 percent of his business in just ninety days. Yikes! Talk about going from the penthouse to the outhouse. **Our goal was:**

- Specific – to cover our bills by identifying financial restructuring and management options

- Measurable – to cover those bills consistently each month

- Achievable – by increasing hours at my work while my husband focused on rebuilding his company

- Realistic – through obtaining coaching via a financial management class and a trained instructor

- Time-bound – by establishing a workable plan for approximately twelve months and then reevaluating our circumstances.

I'm happy to report these S.M.A.R.T. changes worked. Whew! Making some pivots enabled us to successfully cover our financial needs and rebuild my husband's health and wellness corporation. That company, coincidentally named *GoPivot*, is still in business today, weathering the aftermath of the COVID-19 pandemic and finding ways to thrive in another season of challenge.

Many times, the situations we face or the choices we make create problems that don't disappear. And the quicker we take action, the better.

Voicing our challenges, needs, and S.M.A.R.T. goals help us get going in the desired direction! Name it, say it, claim it!

The key component of change is the direction we are going. Ultimately, if we go in the right direction we will become nearer and nearer to where we want to be.

◎ *Final Action Items for Target 1:*

- You are likely considering stepping onto the "S.M.A.R.T. change" path because you have your own issues that haven't gone away. Frame the main challenge you are facing today utilizing S.M.A.R.T. (using the space below)!

- Lastly, take action! Start sharing your target and S.M.A.R.T. objectives with another person this week or at your next group!

Notes to Myself:

Chapter 3

Ndestructible 7 Target #2: Creating the Right Environment!

Armor Up & Hit Target #2!

"Therefore everyone who hears these words of mine and puts them into practice is like a wise man who built his house on the rock." – Matthew 7:24

◎ *Target 2 Reflection:*

Now when Jesus saw the crowds, he went up on a mountainside and sat down. His disciples came to him, and he began to teach them ... He said, regarding the wise and foolish builders ... Therefore everyone who hears these words of mine and puts them into practice is like a wise man who built his house on the rock. The rain came down, the streams rose, and the winds blew and beat against that house; yet it did not fall, because it had its foundation on the rock.

*t everyone who hears these words of mine and
es not put them into practice is like a foolish
m who built his house on sand. The rain came
down, the streams rose, and the winds blew and
beat against that house, and it fell with a great
crash. (Matthew 5:1-2, 7:24-27)*

W hat do we learn from the above? A lot! A critical point is that the right circumstances set us up to thrive or to struggle!

It is our responsibility to ensure that we are living in an environment that empowers us to thrive. Just like a knight wouldn't want to be weighed down by unnecessarily heavy neck or shoulder armor in battle, we don't need to be bogged down from being in the wrong surroundings for too long! It's time to properly equip yourself to fight for the life you deserve.

*I am ready to turn away from the environment that weighed
me down and to create a new environment that will make
this happen!*

For you to maneuver through your troubles and achieve your goals, you need the right set up! So, take a break. Allow for some reflection time. Go on a walk, or sit in a comfortable, quiet area. Chew over the following.

◎ *Initial Exercises for Target 2–Ask Yourself:*

- Are you placing yourself in the right circumstances?

- What surroundings will lead you on your pathway to success?

- Evaluate and explore the current environmental factors that are hindering you: What do you need to eliminate, change, or tweak?

- What will be difficult to change in your surroundings and circumstances?

- Will this impact the key aspects of your life?

- Declare to yourself, *"I will need to make the following changes to have a chance at successfully accomplishing my target!"* List these commitments below.

Notes to Myself:

_____

_____

_____

_____

_____

_____

_____

_____

_____

For optimal mental renewal,
armor up!
The correct environment is like the right battle suit,
protecting the soldier while allowing them to maneuver adequately!

◎ *Next Reflection for Target 2:*

As a way of breaking down key spheres of our lives, consider the following helpful acronym: **SOSPIE** ("SOS" alerts for regular monitoring of the vital slices of "PIE" of our lives). Ask yourself, *"Will I need to make some changes in the below areas to have a chance at successfully accomplishing my needs and/or to lead a life of emotional well-being going forward?"*

- Socially/Relationally: *"Will this affect my social/relational life? Do I have the right social connections/network in place to make this happen? Am I spending enough time with the right people? Am I needing some tips from a peer experienced in what I am handling to get me started? Do I need to inform loved ones? When is the right time to include friends or family?"*

- Occupationally: *"Are there work-life adjustments that I need to make in order for this to take place? Do I have the right work-life balance to make this pan out?"*

- Spiritually/Experientially: *"Have I carved out quiet time and prayer to give me the right perspective? Are there spiritual principles that I've used before that will help me achieve my goal? Am I leveraging quality resources? Am I needing to participate in a group related to what I am handling to persist in this transformation?"*

- Physically: *"Do I have the energy level to pull this off? Am I sleeping enough to be clear? Am I getting in the right nutrition to fuel myself in order to persevere in the days ahead?"*

- Intellectually: *"Do I need to learn something to make this transpire? Do I need to take this on as a hobby first? Am I needing a good step-by-step workbook? Is there a related podcast that will sharpen me and encourage me to continue in this journey?"*

- Emotionally: *"Am I following the stress/anger/time management tips that I already know about? Do I have the right mindset and self-talk to help me carry this out? Do I need to engage in calming techniques to manage my stress while I make this transition?"*

◎ *Next Exercise for Target 2:*

- After contemplating SOSPIE, are their spheres of your life that you need to add, eliminate, change, or tweak? List these needs below.

- Narrow down three to five action items and tell yourself, *"I will take the following steps over the next one to two weeks."* List your steps below.

Notes to Myself:

Chapter 4

Ndestructible 7 Target #3: Choosing New Habits for Progress!

Armor Up & Hit Target #3!
"Start hitting the targets! You, young pups, can be strong, fit warriors for life's troubles ahead. Us old dogs will hit our targets and finish strong!"

◎ *Target 3 Reflection:*

W hen I was an undergrad psychology student, I began studying how habits–good and bad–develop. A pivotal moment in my thinking on this topic occurred when I was about nineteen years old. I participated in a behavioral science experiment involving rats. My assignment was to teach a white rat to press a lever for food and then monitor its behavior based on different feeding schedules. This is called a Skinner Box, or a live operant conditioning chamber experiment, which today is often done through virtual simulation.

It's been decades since I did this work, but I still remember this experiment so vividly! I discovered that the rat would change its behavior based on when the food was delivered. If the food was delivered routinely, the rat would press more slowly. If the food was delivered randomly, the rat would become quite manic, pushing the bar rapidly even when not hungry.

I've come to understand that the rat behaved much like humans, changing its behavior based on different schedules of reinforcement, such as various cues, routines, and payoffs. When we have to make a pivot, it is critical to study ourselves; examining and tracking our own triggers, patterns, and gains!

◎ *Exercises for Target 3:*

Again, pause. Take a break. Get in a safe, quiet space. Enter a period of reflection and self-examination. Follow the exercise below, taking breaks whenever you need to simply speak out loud to yourself. Or, jot down a few commitments or reminders to yourself. Later, consider sharing these contemplations with a trusted loved one or a wise friend.

- Imagine you are a wise friend giving someone you care about advice regarding what you are facing. What advice would you give them? Brainstorm: What are the first one to three considerations/ideas/tips that come to your mind?

- While thinking of your current challenges or problems, ask yourself, *"What's working for me and what isn't?"*

- Examine the "triggers" for your choices or behaviors. What has provoked participation or started this way of going about things?

Ask yourself:

- *"If I keep going down this path, what is likely to happen long-term?"*

- *"How long is an acceptable amount of time to experience this (i.e. grief, sadness, resentment, etc.)?"*

- *"What do I specifically need to drop or stop to end this cycle and when?"*

- *"What are the true benefits of stopping my self-defeating behaviors and 'stinking thinking'?"*

Notes to Myself:

◎ *Next Exercises for Target 3:*

Now it is time to study your obstacles and payoffs!

- **What obstacles have been behind your old habits?**
  Examples:

  - ❖ Ask yourself, *"Do I need to build up first, to get the energy/bandwidth, so I can proceed with taking steps toward meeting my goals or claiming my overall mental wellness?"*

  - ❖ Common obstacles – Our resistance goes up, and our chances of engaging in our healthy behaviors/habits go down, when we are having sensations such as hunger (nutritionally or emotionally), irritation, loneliness or fatigue. Thus, it is very effective to utilize the HALT method to weigh in on any self-care complications you may be experiencing. The HALT method is a technique frequently used in twelve-step programs.[5] The acronym reminds us to stop – or H.A.L.T. – and address everyday triggers that could lower our capacity of taking action in meeting our needs. Thus, HALT and check-in with yourself, *"Am I …*

    - H – hungry?
    - A – angry?
    - L – lonely?
    - T – tired?

❖ Lastly, pause and consider, *"Do I possess any other characteristics – attitudinal, behavioral, lifestyle or otherwise – that are impeding my capacity or motivation to prevail over my challenges?"*

- **Study your payoffs** – What payoffs have been behind your old habits? Examples and considerations:

  ❖ Be brutally honest about automatic payoffs or rewards if you are solving a self-defeating behavior. Ask:

    - *"Is there a short-term payoff that I am experiencing–such as discomfort avoided, emotional release, immediate high, quick reward or some other incentive–preventing me from choosing alternatives?"*

    - *"Despite long-term drawbacks, does my current unwanted habit bring me an immediate emotional need, such as a sense of safety, escape or comfort?"*

  ❖ Examples of payoffs/rewards:

    - *"My anger gets others to stop and at least consider doing what I want or need."*

    - *"My resentment keeps me on guard."*

    - *"I avoid so I don't have to deal with hassles."*

    - *"I isolate so I don't have to cope with others' comments/preferences/opinions."*

- *"Worry makes me feel prepared and in control."*

- **Establish powerful alternatives** – To eliminate a payoff for your undesired behavior, you must come up with alternatives. These behaviors must be equal or more powerful!

  ❖ Examples of effective alternatives:

  - *"Instead of responding in anger, I can be assertive and go for the win-win."*

  - *"I don't need to carry the weight of ongoing resentment to protect myself from the unfairness. For now, I can move on and get my needs met in other ways and by other people."*

  - *"I don't need to automatically avoid this conflict simply because I am having strong and uncomfortable feelings. I can ask a few questions and then decide my next response."*

  - *"Rather than worry, I can truly be in control by waiting to see what actually happens and then deal with the issue if it occurs; sparing myself the ongoing inner turmoil leading up to the matter and given the possibility that what I am anticipating may never occur the way I expect."*

Detailed Example:

Weight loss example (providing a discussion of triggers, patterns, hurdles, and replacements):

- **The triggers/cues**: If you are trying to lose weight, identify what triggers the behaviors you wish to change. You may notice the constant challenge of passing up certain bakery items. Maybe it's simply too tempting to pass up certain items if they are left within sight. Can you pass them by if they are left on the kitchen counter?

- **The routine/rituals/obstacles**: By examining your routines, you come to realize that you cannot pass up certain tasty items when you are hungry (such as treats in the breakroom, the fast-food drive thru on the way to work, or samples in the grocery store). These behaviors directly prevent you from having any self-control.

- **The payoffs/rewards**: There is almost always a "payoff" for your behavior. It can take effort, or sometimes others, to help us figure out what the "reward" is for our self-defeating behavior. In the above example, the payoff for eating the treat in the breakroom could be that it makes you feel more comfortable or gain needed energy for the work ahead of you.

- **The alternatives**: So, our task becomes identifying those enticing and high-powered alternatives. You decide to:

❖ have an appetizing, premade protein smoothie prior to starting work; so you go directly by the break room and proceed to your desk to start the day.

❖ have prepared snacks and meals placed in the refrigerator that will provide true stamina, nourishment, and satisfaction; helping you choose something more beneficial.

❖ pause and pray to make the next choice; this way, you commit to taking food one step at a time and truly discern the next right course of action!

Using new, fitting habits empowers us to walk sure-footed toward a better next chapter!

Notes to Myself:

◎ *Final Exercises for Target 3:*

I realize that to eliminate a payoff for my negative behavior, the reward for a positive behavior must be equal or more powerful! I will choose new habits that will build me up!

To help you follow through with your commitment, respond to the questions below in the notes section.

- What routines or behaviors will help you get what you need and/or want? Why are these equally better, or definitely better, than the old way?

- You can re-embrace old habits you haven't been utilizing. What routines, patterns, or habits have you used in the past? Will they help you meet your goals?

- When reviewing your routines, set practical routines that you can implement; the simpler, the better. ("Don't get too fancy unless you must!"–Lenore.) Ask yourself, *"Am I being realistic?"*

- Develop equal or more powerful alternatives! Ask yourself, *"What top simple/basic two replacement behaviors can I begin to put in place to help me go in the right direction?"*

Notes to Myself:

_____

_____

_____

_____

_____

_____

_____

_____

This R.E.N.E.W.A.L. step is the "sabaton," otherwise known as the armored boots that cover a soldier's feet. Making those smart, fundamental choices protects us and empowers us to walk in the right direction toward achieving new, healthier habits!

Chapter 5

Ndestructible 7 Target #4: Embracing Everlasting Character & Experiences!

Armor Up & Hit Target #4!
"Some of our greatest moments can be broken down by a simple word: joy, courage, goodness, love, favor, compassion, peace, patience, caring, self-control, fortitude, honor, integrity. Against such there is no condemnation! Let us be led by our Holy Spirit!"

◎ *Target 4 Reflection:*

All of us have a unique personality, which is our inner spirit. Our character qualities are at the core of how we make choices and navigate through life. Our internal character influences us to make decisions. The fallout from our behavior does reverberate throughout our life and stare back at us. It's like an echo.

For example, suppose you are kind and respectful to an acquaintance. In that case, they will often reciprocate with attention and regard for you. But if you are experiencing diminished connections and distance from others, you may want to consider what character qualities you are displaying that may be influencing them to distance from you. Intentionally or unintentionally, maybe you are being indifferent, withdrawn, distracted, or showing some other form of separation.

Many have tried to define the core of a good character or good spirit. One of my favorite answers comes from the apostle Paul. He proclaimed, *"The fruit of the Spirit is love, joy, peace, patience, kindness, goodness, faithfulness, gentleness, and self-control" (Gal. 5:22-23).*

Just as the armor's breastplate protects the warrior's vital organs, we must guard what is within our hearts. Choosing the right character and seeking the right experiences naturally helps us create and maintain our emotional well-being!

◎ *Exercises for Target 4:*

I will embrace excellent character traits and experiences that will armor me for the journey! So, pause and reflect on your personality and how you are spending your time. To help you reflect, consider the questions below and then make notes to yourself.

- What three to five personality traits have others told you are strengths of yours?

- Will any of these three to five assets help you with your current challenges and help you navigate effectively ahead?

- Below, list character strengths and virtues that will help you move forward with your needs/goals? Which do you possess?

- Could you benefit from emphasizing certain character traits? Will they help you achieve your target goals and lead a life of mental well-being?

Notes to Myself:

◎ *Next Exercises for Target 4:*

What is the bottom line here? To ensure that you are engaging in experiences that will lead you to achieving your goals, bring peace, and bring emotional well-being for yourself and those around you. Then, everyone wins! Study yourself using the below questions, and then journal your reactions:

- Evaluate and explore your territories and travels. Where and how have you been spending your time?

- Lately, have you been engaged in meaningful, life-giving activities?

- To reach your next goal and to maintain your mental well-being, do you need to pursue a hobby, lead a more active spiritual life, or approach your daily work differently?

Notes to Myself:

_____

_____

_____

_____

_____

_____

_____

Just as the breastplate protects our vital organs, we must, with our decisions and behaviors, guard against what is around us and even within us. Letting in only that which is honorable, admirable, lovely, excellent, and praiseworthy is a crucial filter that makes a massive difference for our R.E.N.E.W.A.L.

◉ *Final Pro Tips for Target 4:*

Selecting the right experiences may sound complicated, but fear not, it can be done!

Don't get too fancy unless you must! Be mindful to include simple, daily wellness actions or acts of kindness. See my list below.

After you review my sample list, make your own list below!

- Take a walk with a family member and share a highlight moment or a stuck point in your journey.

- Place a Post-it note on your bathroom mirror so the first thing you see in the morning will be an inspiring message. This will help you remain on track with your recovery journey.

- Take "time-outs" at least one to two times a day to praise yourself for your progress and to be grateful for your victories and surprises.

- Send a text to a friend letting them know about your recent victory and how much you appreciate them.

- Text a co-worker to let them know how much you've benefited from their support.

- Check in with a group member, opening up about how much they inspire you.

Notes to Myself:

Chapter 6

Ndestructible 7 Target #5: Letting My Wisdom Win!

Armor Up & Hit Target #5!
Jesus said again, "I come that you may have life, and have it to the full." -John 10:10

◎ *Target 5 Reflection:*

You are the manager and director of your life. Doing this job with success entails filtering your experiences, emotions, and thoughts. Effective filtration in this sense requires tapping into our wisdom. Wisdom is the soundness of an action or decision with regard to experience, knowledge, and good judgment.

Wisdom is the shield of our battle suit; it is our protector. Letting our wise mind win empowers us to gain clarity and to make healthier choices.

*Wisdom is the shield of our battle suit—the
protection against life's blows or missiles.
It is meant to prevent us from suffering harm!*

But what do we mean by the "wise mind"? Below is important information and an example to help with comprehending and connecting to your wise mind.

Necessary Information About the Wise Mind:

Here are some essential basics about the concept of wisdom in psychology and in the spirit world:

- **In psychology, wisdom comes from** the process of filtering both our emotions and logic. The "wise mind" is a key concept of D.B.T., or dialectical behavior therapy. It's an approach first developed by Marsha M. Linehan in the late 1980s.[6] In her process, **the wise mind is that place where**

our rational thinking mind and the emotional thinking mind overlap.

❖ It is the synthesis of both emotions and rationality, where we do what works and what is best.

• **In spiritual wisdom**, we allow the Holy Spirit to flow through us through prayer, worship, meditation, study of Scripture, and other faith-oriented practices. Leading a spiritual life nurtures our characters and souls. Wisdom is gained. We sense it, we experience it. We also understand wisdom by allowing Scripture to soak into our minds and hearts. Enlightening scripture, such as:

❖ "How much better to get wisdom than gold, to get insight rather than silver!" (Proverbs 16:16)

❖ "The one who gets wisdom loves life; the one who cherishes understanding will soon prosper." (Proverbs 19:8)

❖ "Be wise in the way you act toward outsiders; make the most of every opportunity. Let you conversation be always full of grace, seasoned with salt, so that you may know how to answer everyone." (Colossians 4:5-6)

❖ "The wisdom from above is first pure, then peaceable, gentle, open to reason, full of mercy and good fruits, impartial and sincere." (James 3:17)

❖ "Do not deceive yourselves. If any of you think you are wise by the standards of this age, you should become fools so that you may become wise." (1 Corinthians 3:18)

❖ "Therefore everyone who hears these words of mind and puts them into practice is like a wise man who built his house on the rock." (Matthew 7:24)

❖ "Fools find no pleasure in understanding but delight in airing their own opinions." (Proverbs 18:2)

❖ "When pride comes, then comes disgrace, but with humility comes wisdom." (Proverbs 11:2)

❖ "Teach us to number our days, that we may gain a heart of wisdom." (Psalm 11:2)

❖ "All this also comes from the Lord Almighty, whose plan is wonderful, whose wisdom is magnificent." (Isaiah 28:29)

Example of the Wise Mind:

Below is a simple example of the difference between the wise mind and other states of mind, such as the logical side of our mind or the emotional/reactive side, using temptation by food, such as chocolate.

Eating chocolate:

- Studies have proven that, when we eat chocolate, our brain releases chemicals such as endorphins or serotonin, which are known to be associated with happiness and overall wellness.[7]

- Emotional or reactive eating involves choosing chocolate whenever we want it. We know it will bring pleasure or soothe us. Yummy!

- Eating, from pure logic, involves selecting food because it's the right nutritional choice for us at any given time, giving us healthy, desired results. Well, chocolate can be high in sugar and saturated fat. It is a high-energy, high-calorie food, and eating a good amount can result in excess weight gain, which is a risk factor for conditions like cardiovascular disease and diabetes.

- **Letting the wise mind win when it comes to chocolate** is a blend of logic and emotion, resulting in a wise choice! It involves the process of discernment. Pausing and pursuing spiritual understanding and guidance may be that vital ingredient to making the best choice for ourselves. So, in this case, **tapping into our wisdom blends our feelings and reasoning and leads to consuming this food item in moderate amounts, which allows for its health benefits and brings satisfaction!**

◎ *Next Reflection for Target 5:*

You've been involved in all of your good choices and also all of your bad ones. You're personally invested in all of your emotional reactions and in all of your emotional overreactions. When facing a predicament, pause and study yourself.

The activities below will help you examine yourself.

- **Be aware of your current natural, raw reactions and emotions**. Our emotions are necessary indicators or signs as to what is happening around us.

  ❖ For example, anger can be an early indicator that something in our life feels outside of our control.
  ❖ Fear is a warning of danger.
  ❖ Guilt indicates perceived wrongdoing.
  ❖ Other core emotions include sadness, disgust, surprise, happiness, or guilt. Emotions give us vital information!

- At the same time, **let your logical thinking kick into gear**. Clarify assumptions and set aside feelings and biases. It is not about going with one's gut. It's about understanding based on facts. It's about making decisions or taking action based on reasoning. Here are some examples of facts in human behavior you may find interesting:

  ❖ Our pupils enlarge when we look at somebody we love.

- ❖ Religious rituals, such as prayer, are associated with significantly lower levels of mental issues or psychological discomfort.
- ❖ Smiling makes people feel happier, scowling makes them feel angrier, and frowning makes them feel sadder.
- ❖ The pain we feel from rejection is akin to physical discomfort.

- **Be mindful!** Begin understanding when your reactionary mind, logical mind, or your wise mind is leading you. Make this a part of your lifestyle.

- **Practice!** Practicing such discernment takes time. To begin with, you may need to pause a little each day while considering job-related or ordinary, everyday troubles you are facing. Rehearsing using this conceptual structure will allow you to weave this framework into the fabric of your personality.

The full, abundant life refers to life in its abounding fullness of joy and strength of spirit, soul, and body. Grounding ourselves in a spirit of wisdom armors us up to do such!

Notes to Myself:

◎ *Final Exercise for Target 5:*

With your present specific tangle(s), first pause and be aware of your various states of mind. Then use the space below for journaling.

- Study yourself! Examine your emotions and logic by taking time to pay attention to these various inner states and to distinguish them from one another!

- Filter! Pause and pray. Talk out loud to yourself. Voice your various feelings and thoughts.

- Take some time. Meditate. Read related scripture. The wise mind has a different flavor, and you will sense its presence; that's the Holy Spirit at work. Without question, when we are filled with the Wise Spirit, we do what's best for ourselves and those around us. Come to know when your wisdom is guiding you!

- Such a conversation usually goes like, *"Lord, part of me feels this way, but my logical side says this ... If I combined my feelings with my logic, it would be hard, but it would leave me with these options ..."*

- If needed, go to your considerate friends for advice on your competing thoughts and feelings.

Notes to Myself:

Chapter 7

Ndestructible 7 Target #6:
Equipping Myself by Allowing
Others to Hold Me Accountable!

Armor Up & Hit Target #6!
"As iron sharpens iron, so one person sharpens another."
(Proverbs 27:17)

◎ *Target 6 Reflection:*

While we can sometimes solve problems, even complicated ones, on our own, the advice and accountability of others is a valuable asset.

Receiving good, helpful information is like soaking up the sunshine on a cold weather day.

According to a study done in March of 2018 by the American Society of Training and Development, or ASTD, you have a 65 percent chance of completing a goal if you commit to someone for accountability. Furthermore, this research concluded that if you have a specific accountability appointment with a person, your chances of success go up to as much as 95 percent.[8]

Isolation, physically or in our head, is often the quickest path to mental illness.

Acknowledging our feelings of powerlessness in certain situations is often the best motivator to be willing to reach out to others. You come to understand that some battles are simply too big to be fought alone. Some circumstances where accountability makes a huge difference include:

- ❖ an overwhelming problem
- ❖ complex or stubborn habits
- ❖ chronic issues
- ❖ "blind spots," where others have pointed out how important it is for you to change your ways, even when you can't see it

Our accountability partners become critical weaponry in our battle arsenal, helping us overcome those lingering issues haunting us!

Our accountability partners become our artillery on our quest to conquer our demons!

◎ *Exercises for Target 6:*

Our accountability partners are vital weaponry! There are those times when the only thing that brings comfort is the soothing, wise words of a loved one. Begin contemplating those who have been effective individuals in your life! Answer the questions below and make notes to yourself regarding enlisting good support for yourself.

- Think of one to three people who would be interested in hearing about you and what you are up to.

- Would you be willing to share your goals and future desires with these individuals?

- Would you be willing to ask them if you can check-in with them periodically to share how things are going?

- Often, gaining an accountability partner is as simple as sharing your goals with someone we trust and asking them to check in routinely so we stay on track.

- Or we can ask them to:

  ❖ push us to set our goals
  ❖ provide interactive feedback regarding how to break down our targets into achievable steps
  ❖ **encourage us to keep going, even if we hit a roadblock**

- **Pro tip! When our accountability partner guides us, make sure you pause and only listen.** Then reflect or ask a question and avoid things like debating.

  ❖ Don't debate! Say, *"That's an important consideration," "I haven't thought of that," "That makes complete sense,"* or *"That's something to think about for sure."*
  ❖ When interacting with an accountability partner, it doesn't mean you agree right then (or ever). You are not obligated to do exactly as they say. What they say can inspire you or give you ideas about other things you can do.

Notes to Myself:

Chapter 8

Ndestructible 7 Target #7: Loving Myself and Others!

Armor Up & Hit Target #7!

"Love never fails. But where there are prophecies, they will cease; where there are tongues, they will be stilled; where there is knowledge, it will pass away."–1 Corinthians 13:4-7

◎ *Target 7 Reflection:*

Ah, love! There are so many kinds of love: self-love, romantic love, charitable love, and so on. Each type can have many different degrees. These feelings of love can be mild, moderate, or intense. They can be warm-hearted or firm, emotional or spiritual.

As humans, we endlessly analyze and pursue love. And still, for all our efforts, it remains an incredibly difficult topic to tackle.

As a verb, love is that deep affection for yourself and others shown through actions such as warmth, tenderness, giving, kindness, listening, devotion, or protection, just to mention a few. In the activities below, we will focus on love in action and some necessities when protecting our relationships, preserving our mental wellness, and giving a big boost to our self-esteem.

Loving one's self and others is like the armored gloves to our battle suit; covering us and enhancing our ability to tend to ourselves and connect to others on a whole new level!

◎ *Reflections for Target 7:*

Call up your loving heart. Do what is best for yourself and those around you! Challenge yourself. In those everyday moments, make a commitment to:

- having a loving and optimistic mindset

- doing a little something for your self-care

- being attentive toward your most important relationships

- being loving in your sphere of influence; your home, work, and community

Unfortunately, there are times when we must battle our basic human nature! It is necessary that each of us beware of enemies, including our own basic natural tendencies that invade our loving intentions toward others and ourselves! Below, you will find what I believe to be the top three self-defeating tendencies of humans. Avoid these traps!

❖ Selfishness/Self-absorption—the preoccupation with one's own activities, thoughts, or interests versus expanding one's views to encompass more people, ideas, or things. According to experts like Gary Chapman (author of The Five Love Languages), *"The attitude of selfishness is natural … the attitude of love is not natural."*[9]

❖ Negativity Bias[10] — a phenomenon where we emphasize unpleasant experiences. Negative occurrences naturally stick with us. As an example, presume that you spent a few, mostly positive, days with a family member. But at some point, this person said something offensive to you. Now, you categorize the entire experience as negative; rather than balancing your thinking with the many highlights that happened during the trip.

• Inattention to Self-care — Do not get trapped in self-neglect. "You can't give away what you do not have," or "Put your own oxygen mask on first." The common denominator in both of these metaphors is that you have to take care of yourself before you can take care of others.

I get that we are people of self-preservation, falling into patterns of self-absorption and negativity, all in an effort to be alert and protective of ourselves. But an advanced Ndestructible Warrior is aware of their selfishness and other unhealthy dynamics. On top of that, the Ndestructible Warrior works toward transforming self-defeating tendencies. For example, "Saying what we mean without saying it meanly," rather than being excessively negative. We discipline ourselves to take care of ourselves, so we can better care for others. Focusing on acts of love toward ourselves and others is a key toward the ultimate transformation into being our best self.

◎ *Action Items for Target 7:*

Are any of the above self-defeating tendencies in play in your current life and present challenges?

- Write these tendencies below, and then journal alternatives that you will choose to quickly redirect from them!

- Add the following daily reflection to your mental wellness toolbox to assist you in maintaining an active, loving spirit!

Lord, today I will SERVE.

Self-love   I am kind to myself, as a loving parent would be to their child;

Engage   I look for opportunities to engage with others in a caring manner, even when I don't want to

Readily   I readily look for opportunities to serve in my surroundings in a loving capacity

View   I see things from a perspective of "win-win", doing what is best for all involved

Effect   I impact my community in a manner that leaves a loving, positive mark and legacy

Amen!

Notes to Myself:

Chapter 9

Ndestructible 7 Warrior Groups

"I know what it is to be in need, and I know what it is to have plenty. I have learned the secret of being content in any and every situation, whether well fed or hungry, whether living in plenty or in want. I can do all things through the Lord who gives me strength." -Philippians 4:12-13.

Reflection:

The most efficient route to incorporate *Ndestructible 7* into your life is to participate in or form an *Ndestructible 7* group. So, why a group? And what happens in an *Ndestructible 7* Warrior group?

Before these questions are answered, let me first ask you: Have ever participated in some sort of group experience in your lifetime? If so, what's coming to mind?

I'm hypothesizing that, at least initially, you were nervous about joining, intimidated by putting yourself out there to others, hoping you would be liked, and eager to make a friend. Then the journey continued onward. I'm now guessing that there were awkward moments and amazing moments.

The truth is, there are certain sets of healing factors in play when doing group work.

In Yalom's classic work, Irvin Yalom, an American existential psychiatrist and emeritus professor of psychiatry at Stanford University, identified eleven primary "therapeutic factors" in group therapy.[11]

Each of the "curative factors" Yalom identified helped explain why group experiences enhance recovery for those suffering with addiction.[12] Examples of Yalom's factors include:

1. instillation of hope,
2. universality,
3. encounters with individuals facing similar problems,
4. interpersonal learning input and output,
5. guidance,
6. catharsis,
7. self-understanding,
8. and other existential factors.

In *Ndestructible 7* mental wellness groups, there are regular opportunities for corrective experiences for those of us who participate in such journeys! Here's our top seven:

1. **Inner Spirit Shifts** – Hope, energy, motivation, and fortitude readily and quickly emerge as group members' stories resonate with us; analogously, fueling our personal engine for a much-needed, and often long overdue, change.

2. **"Aha!" Mindset Shifts Quickly** – Learning from others imparts insights/information and furthers our

self-understanding; thus, corrective experiences swiftly emerge for ourselves.

3. **Supportive Network/Community** – Member interactions create a unique bond and an opportunity to have a "second family" within a spirit of mental well-being and caring for others; likewise, we experience love directly.

4. **"Isolation solved!"** – Attending groups provides instant relief from our mental and physical isolation/ withdrawal; hence, keeping us from letting our challenges overshadow us and linger.

5. **"We like people with skills!"** – New Skills – As we witness strengths in others, they naturally become role models for us where we, in turn, can practice these traits in group; therefore, empowering ourselves with new abilities to take with us and use in other instances.

6. **"Say it, claim it!"** – Accountability – We remain on track by voicing our challenges and targets, which also creates opportunity for others to check-in with us later to see how things are going for us; consequently, tackling our common negative human tendencies such as avoidance, escape or procrastination,

7. **"After the Test comes the Testimony!"** – Existential Reality – We connect to others having relatable hurt, upset and adversity who are finding meaning and purpose in their hardship and challenges; accordingly,

awakening us to the realities of our own story for which we can later recount (for our own, or others, benefit).

Through group experience, the number of mental shifts, speed of behavioral pivots, and quick turns toward emotional well-being is quite a phenomenon. Show up and win in the next chapter of your life!

Notes to Myself:

Chapter 10

Ndestructible 7 Group Warrior Oath of FAITH and Group Pro Tips

"If you can't be kind, at least be vague."–Judith Martin

Reflection:

"I don't want to go to a group!" This is a common stance I hear from individuals. On the flip side, I hear most often, *"I am so glad I finally went to a group. It's the best thing I've ever done for my recovery,"* and *"Through the group, I've made the most amazing changes in my life. I've gotten through barriers I've never been able to get through before!"*

With *Ndestructible 7* groups, we encourage awareness of the resistance and rewards of the group. On top of that, our leaders are expected to spend a lot of time setting up each group to have effective interactions and safety. We want pro group members!

Above is such an interesting quote from Judith Martin, better known by the pen name "Miss Manners," a columnist and etiquette authority for a number of decades. What a provoking thought. For our purposes, we want *Ndestructible 7* group warriors to consider etiquette and expectations so that they will have exceptional group interaction.

Below, you will find the *Ndestructible 7 Oath of FAITH.* This oath serves as a guide for group members' mindsets and behaviors. It helps us eliminate "group noise," which is the unnecessary unpleasantness that certain group members often unknowingly exhibit if not oriented to effective group etiquette.

It's so important to periodically review the *Ndestructible 7 Oath of FAITH* in a way that's suitable to the particular needs of the group you are leading. The oath can be communicated a variety of ways such as during a member orientation, through content on a website, in an email, or live in group meeting. Reviewing the oath is necessary when a group member joins, and creativity is often welcome by group participants when covering this material!

- *Keep in mind that participating in a support group is often new, unusual, and intimidating for most people! This oath serves as an important guide for the new group member.*

- *Even for experienced group members, most have never been given detailed instruction on effective group member interaction (unless they have participated in groups, such as twelve-step).*

- *The oath of FAITH briefs every Ndestructible 7 participant regarding expectations, creating safety and comfort.*

Ndestructible 7 Oath of FAITH

T he following *Ndestructible 7 Oath of FAITH* guides the warrior during the group process. It armors group participants with great group member skills, endurance, and fortitude. It helps the group members have F.A.I.T.H. while in the midst of the *Ndestructible 7* quests and challenges.

◎ Faith: Nd7 Group Faith – *We ...*
   - have unbreakable faith in the healing factors that group processes uniquely possess
   - have fortitude and belief in the process, despite the frustrations and setbacks
   - do not "fix" others – we listen and reflect, "soaking in" over time; we learn tools to help ourselves and our situations, letting the ways of Holy Spirit's presence move within us, all of which keeps us on the path to emotional well-being
   - walk by faith and not sight (2 Cor. 5:7) – we are looking for the unseen, divine possibilities that come from the whole journey

◎ Acceptance: Nd7 Group Member Acceptance – *We ...*

- are grace-filled – *Ndestructible 7* groups are a "blended family" membership
- are intrigued and curious of faith differences and the paths that others walk
- give each other space and time for discovery of what is best for us and to own our own faults
- accept that no recovery program, including this one, is perfect – there will be ups and downs
- trust and help our leader – we readily take any concerns to the group leader; we will allow our leadership to respond to safety issues
- provide Grace – *"Where the Bible speaks, we speak; where the Bible is silent, we are silent"* (Thomas Campbell, 1809); Scripture is our inspiration; we honor Scripture, and we also know it's a complicated matter to interpret Scripture; if confused or frustrated with an interpretation communicated during a group encounter, confide in other spiritual mentors and your leader privately after the group meeting.

◎ Intentions: Nd7 Group Member Intentions – *We ...*
- monitor our intentions – intentions matter; we monitor our objectives when speaking; are we supporting? Sharing? Lecturing?
- do not debate – we wonder; we are curious; we reflect; we consider; we give consideration; we allow for grace/ space/time

- share airtime during sharing times – sharing in concise segments; we use one to four minutes for our sharing (unless another time frame is given/requested)
- self-regulate – sharing our feelings is expected; nonverbals, such as grief, tears, and sadness, are all welcome, but we do not curse or yell, as this can be misunderstood and quickly activate/elevate ourselves and others
- are self-referred and self-motivated – we are not a required group, such as court-ordered or family-ordered; if your energy is down, pause before group to move into the right mental spirit by listening to music, reviewing devotionals, or praying; the leader will sign in at least five minutes early for reflection/greeting/chatting

◎ Togetherness: Nd7 Group Togetherness – *We ...*
- **USE VALIDATING REFLECTION** – brief, validating statements, verbal hugs, and nonverbal interest and caring, such as:
  - † *"Great courage,"* or *"Great strength withstanding those circumstances."*
  - † *"That's a tough situation,"* or *"Way to handle this challenge."*
  - † *"You're clearly doing your best,"* or *"Your story inspires me."*
  - † *"That makes sense,"* or *"That makes complete sense."*
- tap into our wisdom – monitoring our emotions and avoiding reactions; understanding that validation doesn't mean you completely agree, but you might; validating means you are with the other person and allows

for that space and growth of the witnesses; respecting that others walk their own path

- do not go back and forth – we avoid cross-talk exchange, such as back-and-forth communication between dyads/triads, nonverbal transfer signals, clearly casual conversation, or therapy/treatment-like/advice-giving exchange from one individual to another
- promptly admit mistakes – when we recognize we are straying from the oath, we promptly admit the mistake and redirect
- use the chat feature and use others' first names
- encourage frustration/anger to be checked with the group leadership – the processing of these feelings is done over time and with thoughtfulness, not reaction; this usually becomes clearer in between group sessions and in private first; irritability/agitation signal that you are wrestling with something within yourself and/or in the group; if needed, check your frustration with the leader; most importantly, plan to communicate by saying what you mean without saying it meanly

◎ Healing: Nd7 Group Member Healing – *We ...*
- allow for the material to speak for itself – the steps/targets will speak to us and heal us at a time that is right or appropriate for us
- recognize that our symptoms speak to our needs – for example, grief signals hurt and the need for comfort; anger signals a need to solve helplessness and a need to gain empowerment; depression signals haplessness and the need to bring hope/faith/joy/contentment; burnout

signals being overwhelmed and need for rejuvenation/ refreshment/regeneration (etc.)

- honor that **MENTAL WELLNESS is our focus** – we work on meeting our needs in the here and now, rather than becoming excessively focused on the symptoms and stuck in our problems; we are moving from existing to shining, from surviving to thriving in the day-to-day, from letting life deal with us to taking charge of our life
- pause if we believe the group is preventing our healing – we promptly share these concerns to the instructor in a private, timely manner soon after the meeting
- allow for group mentors and a mentorship program – leaders of groups can develop a mentorship program within their group to promote further support and healing (Note: eligibility to serve as a mentor for other participants in a group will be based on such criteria as successful completion of one round of the *Ndestructible 7* process – completing all seven targets for a particular hurt, wound or impairment – with success and quality group participation prior to applying to be a mentor for others)

Pro Group Agenda and Member Tips

B elow is a sample group agenda, including etiquette reminders for virtual video conferencing groups. Such agendas and reminders allow for people to be pro group members and to have pro group experiences.

◎ **Announcements and Etiquette Pro Reminders for Virtual Video Conferencing Groups** (display or review the below live) – **Remember to …**
  - Participate in a private environment – make certain your space assures confidentiality for other group members so only you hear and see the live interactions and others (it is essential that others – such as roommates, family members, and others in nearby rooms – cannot see or hear the meeting)
  - Give it your all – give yourself the full time for your self-care; put cell phone on "Do not disturb" and inform family in advance not to interrupt
  - Be on camera – be engaging with nonverbal interaction; however, turn off your camera if addressing an urgent issue
  - Presentation – nice casual or dressy workout attire is best

- Sign in four to five minutes early – test your connection and sound; enter a spirit of reflection
- Limit distractions – avoid eating, chewing gum, snacking, and vaping; these activities impact your and others' ability to be present; drinks or smoothies work best.

◎ **Prayers** (have group members read at least the two prayers below) – *Let us pray …*
  1. *Group Member's Covenant Commitment*
     – found on page 9
  2. *Armor-up for Renewal: Ndestructible 7*
     – found on page 10
     - † which includes the seven targets for emotional well-being
     - † is a blend of spirituality, behavioral science, and life experiences
     - † starts your new chapter as you begin hitting the targets

◎ *Ndestructible 7 Group Warrior Oath of FAITH*–review all or parts as is suitable for the various group meetings

◎ **Today's lesson** – review a target, present a topic or lesson, and/or have a speaker (i.e., providing a brief testimony, sharing a breakthrough or victory, or presenting a relevant topic)

◎ **Group Sharing – following the group tips found on pages 100-105**

◎ **Closing Prayers – using the prayers found on pages 113-115**

◎ **Homework suggestions**
1) Let today's group experience soak in by taking a few quiet moments to reflect in a comfortable spot or share with a mentor (while honoring the principle of ano-nymity to avoid identifying other group members)
2) Pause throughout the week, one or two times a day. Breathe and reflect by talking to yourself. Write a letter or note to yourself. Or, journal about anything that is a key consideration for you right now
3) Continue refining your next actions
4) Practice your new thinking and behaviors
5) Notice if any newness is already present

Notes to Myself:

Conclusion

Ndestructible 7 Closing Prayers and Messages

Ndestructible 7 **Warrior Prayer of Conviction**

As a warrior, I navigate the journeys ahead,
following my brave heart,
tackling life's inevitable troubles,
honoring the wisdom that comes from above,
serving courageously, and
living life to the fullest!

Ending Reflection:

We all get off track at times in our lives. We all have experienced wrecks, been broken down, and have had clean-up to do. *Ndestructible 7* gives us those key foundational targets that can help us improve ourselves and our situations.

The theory behind *Ndestructible 7* is "if we change, things will change!" Our seven targets equip us for life's battles ahead.

My hope is that you will protect yourself better, recover from anything life throws at you, and be better equipped to fight for yourself and those around you. *Ndestructible 7* is a gift to you so you can "armor up" and optimize the coming chapters of your life.

You are the best person to look after yourself! Protect yourself! And stay in touch with the Mighty Warrior!

By asking for divine intervention and protection, you will connect with the Mighty Warrior. Add the following blessing to your arsenal to make for a closer relationship with our Mighty Warrior.

The *Ndestructible 7* Blessing

Lord, You are the Mighty Warrior fighting for me.
Your miracles are welcome!
Your warriors slay giants with unexpected and unusual weapons.
Do Your mighty work within me!

I will notice Your divine moments & direction;
I will not limit You!
Lord, You told me that You desire for me to live life to the fullest,
abounding in joy and strength of character.
I will receive Your blessings, even when I am weak and
undeserving!
I know You are near
and are with me wherever I go!

Finish strong! Some of our greatest moments can be broken down by a simple word: joy, courage, goodness, love, favor, compassion, peace, patience, caring, self-control, fortitude, honor, integrity. Against such, there is no condemnation! Let us be led by our Holy Spirit!

Take care of yourself! Put the Lord on speed dial! I believe the Lord is waiting for your call. God wants to show up and bless you.

We began our journey in a spirit of belief. We end our journey by having an exceptional suit of armor. I pray that good things come your way!

For your final send-off, I offer you the Aaronic Blessing (Num. 6:22-27):

May the Lord bless you and keep you;
May the Lord make His face shine upon you,
And be gracious to you;
May The Lord lift up His countenance upon you,
And give you peace.
- The Holy Bible

About the Author

Dr. Lenore Lawson Doster, MA, PsyD

D<!---->r. Doster is a licensed clinical psychologist and mental wellness consultant. She specializes in virtual services, making mental health and mental wellness processes accessible and readily available.

Her career is dedicated to:

Psychotherapy for

- young adults and adults (ages eighteen and older) in a life transition or in need of increased coping/management of life's challenges (relational, school, work/career, emotion/anger regulation, etc.)

- women's issues – relational, work/life balance, and mind/body/spirit issues (including weight maintenance and eating disorders)

- couples – marital enrichment, premarital counseling, relational assessment, relational distress, and anger management

- family and parent consultation – Lenore is the author of *Rock Solid Parenting: Secrets of an Effective Parent*[13]

Mental Wellness Coaching or Consultation for Individuals and Corporations

- providing virtual group services or web conferencing

- utilizing the concepts of *Ndestructible 7: A Rock Solid Path to a Better Life*[14]

Letter from Dr. Doster:

As a clinical psychologist, I am interested in helping with the renewal and transformation of one's mind and spirit to increase peace and contentment. A sense of renewal comes from sharpening one's mindset, coping, and lifestyle throughout the phases of one's life. My practice is primarily through web services to make mental health and mental wellness processes accessible and readily available.

When our everyday relationships and experiences in life at home, work, and/or school bring challenge, change, or adversity, it is natural to experience mental states such as anxiety, stress, depression, and anger. It is up to us to take charge of our cognitive and emotional processes before more life difficulties start. Sometimes, it is time to reach out to a professional for help or to seek a powerful type of support in a group setting, which only group membership can provide.

I began intensive study of the behavioral sciences when I entered into the field of mental health and wellness as an undergraduate psychology student in 1984 at Colorado State University. It was through intensive course study, lab research, mental health service, and advanced degrees (master's and doctorate) that I came to understand the true value of behavioral science models of change. I utilize these models when working with individuals while studying one's thinking, behaviors, relational skills, and life patterns (models such as cognitive behavioral therapy (CBT), mindfulness, existential psychotherapy, positive psychology, or dialectical behavior therapy (DBT)). However, my focus is to meet clients where they are and utilize these models in an effective context for each individual I serve. Thus, I take into account each person's cultural background, family history, spiritual/religious orientation, and faith-based values in order to guide our work.

My advanced training includes:

- Doctorate of Psychology (PsyD) – focus: clinical psychology, doctorate completed October 2002, Georgia School of Professional Psychology at Argosy University

- Master of Arts (MA) – focus: clinical psychology, master's completed 1999, Georgia School of Professional Psychology at Argosy University

- Master of Arts (MA) – focus: higher education administration (student affairs), completed 1990, The Ohio State University

- Bachelor of Science (BS) – focus: psychology/ behavioral science, completed 1988, Colorado State University

My work history includes:

- Psychological Consultative Examiner – The Mpowerment Alliance, Griffin, Georgia (current) and Highlands Professional Group, LLC, Murfreesboro, Tennessee

- Corporate Mental Wellness Consultant – GoPivot, A Company Providing Complete Corporate Wellness, Safety and Engagement Solutions, Atlanta, Georgia (current)

- Psychotherapist and Clinical Coordinator – The Summit Counseling Center, Johns Creek, Georgia

- Psychotherapist – Atlanta Center for Eating Disorders, Atlanta, Georgia

- Doctoral Resident – Philhaven Psychiatric Hospital, Mt. Gretna, Pennsylvania

- Crisis Hotline Phone Service, Training, Management – Colorado State University

My deep faith, spirituality, and interest in international culture comes from a variety of experiences:

- Free Chapel, Gainesville, GA – church member since 2021

- Mount Pisgah United Methodist, Alpharetta, Georgia – church member since 2003–2020

- Philhaven Psychiatric Hospital, Mt Gretna, Pennsylvania – integrative behavioral health doctoral residency with a focus in Christian faith & theology, American Psychological Association accredited, completed 2002

- Recovery of Hope – intensive couples therapy, co-therapist, Philhaven Psychiatric Hospital, 2002

- Peachtree Christian Church, Disciples of Christ, Atlanta – Deacon, member 1990 – 2003

- Atlanta Committee for the Olympic Games – assistant housing manager, Olympic Village, 1996

- SportsNet – Youth Enrichment Through Sports, Inc. – executive director, The Salvation Army, 1995 – 1996

- International Housing Coordinator – Georgia Institute of Technology, 1993 – 1995

Highlights from my early life and current life:

Raised in Colorado, I appreciated adventures such as 4-H, rodeos, cattle drives, and basketball. Now, I'm thrilled when doing outdoor recreation, especially camping and attending college sporting events. My greatest blessings have come from being a Christian, wife, mom, and mother-in-law.

Endnotes

1. Jentezen Franklin, Kingdom Connection Daily Devotional March – May 2023 (Jentezen Franklin Media Ministries, Celebration, Inc., 2023).

2. Lenore Lawson Doster, Rock Solid Parenting: Secrets of an Effective Parent (Maitland, Fla.: Xulon, 2008), https://www.amazon.com/SOLID-PARENTING-Lenore-Lawson-Doster/dp/1604778946/ref=sr_1_1?crid=2SX-WSUCAMF1GY&keywords=rock+solid+parenting+le-nore+doster&qid=1684635169&sprefix=rock+solid+par-enting+lenore+doster%2Caps%2C82&sr=8-1 or https://www.barnesandnoble.com/s/lenore%20Doster

3. George T. Doran, "There's a S.M.A.R.T. Way to Write Management's Goals and Objectives," Management Review 70, 35-36 (1981).

4. John Boitnott, "What Are SMART Goals and How You Can Set and Achieve Them?" Entrepreneur, last modified November 25, 2019, https://www.entrepreneur.com/article/342898

5. Susanne Reed, PhD, "How Using the HALT Concept Prevents Alcohol Relapse," Alcoholics Resource Center, last modified March 9, 2022, https://alcoholicsanonymous.com/how-using-the-halt-concept-prevents-alcohol-relapse/

6. Marcia M. Linehan, DBT® Skills Training Handouts and Worksheets (Second Edition) (New York: Guilford Press, 2015).

7. Daphnée Poupon, "For The Love of Chocolate," Research Outreach, July 1, 2022, https://researchoutreach.org/blog/love-chocolate/

8. Barrett Wissman, "An Accountability Partner Makes You Vastly More Likely to Succeed," Entrepreneur, last modified March 20, 2018, https://www.entrepreneur.com/article/310062

9. Dr. Gary Chapman, Understanding and Expressing Love: Better Together, Free Chapel Service, February 26, 2023, https://www.youtube.com/live/8QeSqJYZzug?feature=share

10. Margaret Jaworski, "What is the Negativity Bias? How Can You Overcome It?" Psycom, last modified February 19, 2020, https://www.psycom.net/negativity-bias

11. Irvin Yalom, The Theory and Practice of Group Psychotherapy, (Basic Books, 1995).

12. Next Step Therapy, "Yalom's Therapeutic Factors," 2023, https://nextsteptherapy.ie/groups/group-psychotherapy/yaloms-therapeutic-factors-2/

13. Lenore Lawson Doster, Rock Solid Parenting: Secrets of an Effective Parent (Maitland, Fla.: Xulon, 2008), https://www.amazon.com/SOLID-PARENTING-Lenore-Lawson-Doster/dp/1604778946/ref=sr_1_1?crid=2SX-WSUCAMF1GY&keywords=rock+solid+parenting+lenore+doster&qid=1684635169&sprefix=rock+solid+parenting+lenore+doster%2Caps%2C82&sr=8-1 or https://www.barnesandnoble.com/s/lenore%20Doster

14. Lenore Lawson Doster, Ndestructible 7: A Rock Solid Path to a Better Life (Maitland, Fla.: Xulon, 2021), https://www.amazon.com/s?k=lenore+doster&i=strip-books&crid=U4A886HAHKTS&sprefix=lenore+doster%2Cstripbooks%2C67&ref=nb_sb_nossor or https://www.barnesandnoble.com/s/lenore%20Doster

Appendix

Main Prayers & Blessings

Armor-up at any time through prayer and reflection! Use the *Ndestructible 7 Covenant Commitment*, the *Armor-up for Renewal: Ndestructible 7 prayer, The Ndestructible 7 Blessing, and/or the Aaronic blessing* (Num. 6:22-27)!

Let us pray ...

Ndestructible™ 7 Covenant Commitment: Forging a great suit of armor!

There are times when I'm at my best. There are times when I'm at my worst. I will handle the baggage I've been carrying. I will prepare for the troubles ahead. I will learn what is best for my well-being here and now. I will armor myself to improve my situation. I will reach for the stars, receive winks from above, and partner with the Holy Spirit. I will hit my targets. I will have a new story!

Armor-up for Renewal: Ndestructible™ 7

Ready, Lord, to put off my old ways and fix my eyes on what is better;
to turn away from the **e**nvironment that weighed me down and broke me;
to walk with **n**ew habits that will build me up;
to let **e**verlasting experiences and excellent character rest on my shoulders;
to allow my **w**isdom to win and shield me from further harm;
to let others equip me and hold me **a**ccountable;
to reach out in acts of **l**ove toward others and myself."

The Ndestructible 7 Blessing

Lord, You are the Mighty Warrior fighting for me.
Your miracles are welcome!
Your warriors slay giants with unexpected and unusual weapons.
Do Your mighty work within me!
I will notice Your divine moments & direction;
I will not limit You!
Lord, You told me that You desire for me to live life to the fullest, abounding in joy and strength of character.
I will receive Your blessings, even when I am weak and undeserving!
I know You are near
and are with me wherever I go!

Aaronic blessing

May the Lord bless you and keep you;
May the Lord make His face shine upon you,
And be gracious to you;
May The Lord lift up His countenance upon you,
And give you peace.
(Numbers 6:22-27)

Take care of yourself! Put the Lord on speed dial!
I believe the Lord is waiting for your call.

Printed in the USA
CPSIA information can be obtained
at www.ICGtesting.com
LVHW022022310124
770457LV00016B/143